THE STARS IN SUMMER

NORTHERN HORIZON

Pole Star

EASTERN HORIZON

WESTERN HORIZON

SOUTHERN HORIZON

See inside back cover for Latin names

This book makes star-gazing much more interesting. Even if you have no binoculars or telescope, you can still enjoy identifying the constellations and their important stars.

This book shows the figures and animals associated with the legends of the stars. Having a mental picture of these makes identification easier.

INDEX

Although the stars are shown in their correct relative positions, some of the old constellation figures have been changed in outline where this makes the shape easier to identify.

THE STARS
and their legends

by ROY WORVILL, M.Sc.

with illustrations by ROBERT AYTON

Publishers: Ladybird Books Ltd . Loughborough
© Ladybird Books Ltd 1973
Printed in England

January

The first month of the year often brings clear, frosty evenings, a good time to look at the stars. The most brilliant star-groups, or constellations as they are called, can be seen now.

Auriga – the Charioteer or the Waggoner

If you live in the earth's northern hemisphere you will find a very bright star overhead in the evening sky. This is *Capella*, a name which means Little She-goat. Old star maps show *Auriga* as a man holding a horse's reins in his right hand with a goat and two small kids cradled by his left arm.

The Arabs, who gave us many interesting star legends and names, called *Capella* 'the Driver' because it was seen before the sky became dark enough to show the fainter stars around it. It is not easy to trace the shape of the Charioteer, but the stars could also seem to follow the shape of a head with a pointed helmet and you might recognise this more easily. The three small stars in the form of a triangle below *Capella* are sometimes called the *Kids*.

Camelopardalis – the Giraffe

Following a line northwards from *Capella* you will see a row of rather faint stars pointing down to the northern horizon. These are part of *Camelopardalis – the Giraffe*. Most of the constellation shapes are very old, but this one was given its name only three centuries ago. Some people said that it was not a giraffe, but the camel on which Rebecca rode to meet Isaac, as the Bible story tells us in the book of Genesis.

(above) Auriga – the Charioteer and star map,
(below) Camelopardalis – the Giraffe and star map.

4

0 7214 0348 4

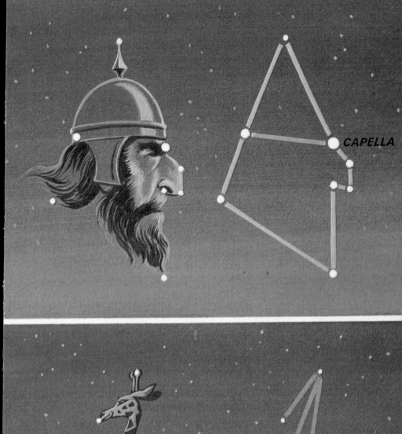

CAPELLA

Orion – the Hunter

The stars of *Orion* make up the most brilliant constellation of the winter sky. You will have no difficulty in tracing the shape of the Hunter, with his shining belt, if you look towards the south in the late evening. *Orion* is mentioned in the Bible and was referred to by the Greek poet, Homer.

The red star at Orion's right shoulder (on the left as you face him), is *Betelgeuse* (pronounced 'Beetle-jooze'). Another very bright star, *Rigel*, marks his left foot. He has a splendid belt of three stars in a sloping line, and his sword hangs from this. Around the middle star of the three in the sword is the misty spot marking the enormous gas-cloud of the *Great Orion Nebula*. You can just see this as faint mist around the star.

The small group of *Lepus – the Hare*, crouches below Orion's feet.

Taurus – the Bull

Orion is supposed to be holding his shield in his left hand to protect himself from the sharp horns of *Taurus – the Bull*. *Taurus* is one of the twelve zodiac star-groups.

Taurus – the Bull has two beautiful star-clusters, the V-shaped *Hyades* and the little group of the *Seven Sisters* or *Pleiades*.

Taurus – the Bull, Orion – the Hunter and (below) Lepus – the Hare.

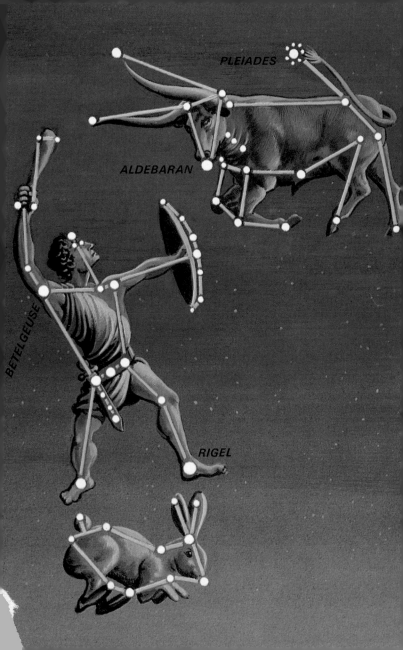

PLEIADES

ALDEBARAN

BETELGEUSE

RIGEL

February

In February the evenings are occasionally fine and clear. Here are the stars to look for.

The two Dogs

The Big Dog, Canis Major, follows close at the heels of *Orion*. It was said to be *Orion's* hunting dog. In this constellation you will soon spot the most brilliant star in the sky, *Sirius*, often called 'the Dog Star'. Thousands of years ago in Egypt, *Sirius* was called *Sothis*. It was worshipped because, when it was seen rising in the eastern sky just before the sun, the people knew that the River Nile would begin to flood over its banks and bring water to their parched land. *Sirius* is one of the nearer stars and this partly explains its great brilliance.

The Little Dog, Canis Minor, is not so conspicuous, but you will find it in line with *Orion's* shoulders, to the left.

The brightest star in this constellation is *Procyon*, a name which means 'the leading dog' and which was probably given because this star rises well before *Sirius* and its companions. Because it lies near the edge of the *Milky Way*, which ancient peoples thought resembled a stream or river, the *Little Dog* has sometimes been called 'the Water Dog'.

An old Arab legend tells that *Sirius* and *Procyon* were two sisters of a young prince who married and travelled to the far southern world. They followed him, but only the elder was strong enough to cross the river of the *Milky Way*. The younger, *Procyon*, was left on the northern bank of the river.

(above) The Big Dog and star plan,
(below) The Little Dog and star plan.

SIRIUS

PROCYON

Gemini – the Twins

The two bright stars of *Gemini* are *Castor* and *Pollux*. When they are rising in the east, *Castor* leads the way up from the horizon and *Pollux*, which is slightly brighter, follows it. Although we see *Castor* as a single star, a large telescope will show it as two. There are others which cannot be seen, for *Castor* is really made up of six stars.

Castor and *Pollux* were the twin heroes of many famous battles in the legends of the Greeks and Romans. They were also believed to be the special guardians of sailors and, in the Bible, we can read how St. Paul travelled from the island of Malta to Rome in a ship which had the Twins as a 'sign' or figure-head. It was among the stars of *Gemini* that the great astronomer Sir William Herschel discovered the planet Uranus when he was observing this part of the sky in March, 1782.

The Milky Way passes by the feet of the Twins, and a pair of binoculars or a small telescope will show some of its crowded star-clusters.

The Lynx

Above the Twins, overhead in the sky, are the faint stars which make up the *Lynx*. It is one of the constellations invented by an astronomer named Hevelius about three centuries ago. It is said that he must have given it this name because anyone who can see its stars clearly has eyesight as keen as that of a lynx!

(above) The Lynx and star plan,
(below) Castor and Pollux and star plan.

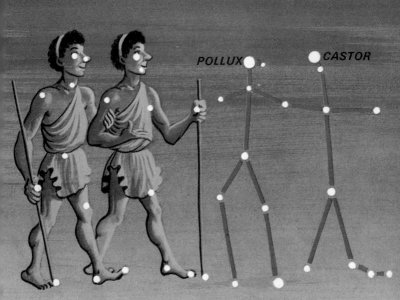

POLLUX　　CASTOR

March

Cancer – the Crab

This constellation is one of the zodiac star-groups. At first it is not easy to see the shape of the Crab; perhaps that is why the people of Egypt called it a beetle, and in India it was referred to as a tortoise.

Its stars are rather faint, but you may be able to see some of them lying to the east of *Castor* and *Pollux*.

Over three centuries ago the great Italian scientist, Galileo, who was the first man to use a telescope to look at the stars, told of his pleasure and surprise when he saw that the misty patch was separated into more than forty points of light. There are, in fact, more than four hundred stars in this cluster and they belong to a kind of stellar family, moving together through space.

An interesting old name and a very suitable one, too, formerly used in England for the faint cluster called *Praesepe* (shown opposite in the upper part of the constellation), is the *Beehive*. If you look at it with a small telescope, or a pair of binoculars, you will see why the comparison is a good one. Many of the stars in this cluster are double or triple and most are of a yellowish-white colour.

Cancer – the Crab and star plan.

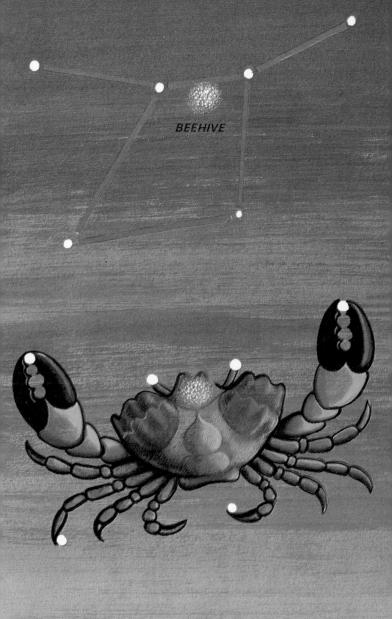

BEEHIVE

Hydra – the Water Snake

Many old stories and legends are about serpents and dragons, so it is not surprising that in the past these were also associated with stars.

The longest of these snakes is *Hydra – the Water Snake*. It stretches about a third of the way across the sky, although it is rather low and often hidden by trees or buildings. The head of *Hydra* lies not far beneath the stars of the *Crab*. Some distance below, at the beginning of the long, winding coils, is *Hydra's* only bright star. It is well-named, *Alphard*, which means the lonely or solitary one.

On its back the *Water Snake* carries two smaller constellations, called *Corvus – the Crow or Raven*, and *Crater – the Cup*, which are best seen in late April or May. One old legend tells that the *Raven* was a favourite bird of the god, Apollo. One day, Apollo sent it to fetch water from a distant fountain. On the journey back the *Raven* loitered, and its late arrival so angered the god that he not only turned its silver plumage to black but placed it in the sky with the *Cup* just out of its reach, so that the thirsty bird could never reach it. The *Raven* was so deeply disgraced that even the timid *Hare* would have nothing to do with it. The stars of the little constellation of *Lepus – the Hare*, sink below the horizon as *Corvus* rises, for – legend tells – the *Hare* tries to keep out of earshot of the *Raven's* croaking voice.

* To see the constellation as it actually appears this month, turn the page slightly clockwise.

ALPHARD

April

Leo – the Lion

In April one of the most splendid of the star-groups can be seen in the southern evening sky – the zodiac constellation of *Leo – the Lion*. It is much more impressive than the little form of *Cancer – the Crab*. Facing south you will soon see the brilliant Sickle of Leo, like a question mark turned from left to right, or resembling a reaper's sickle with the curve of the blade open towards the right. The curved line of the blade is part of the lion's head and shoulders, as you can see in the illustration opposite. The very bright star at the lower end of the handle is called *Regulus*, meaning 'the Little King'.

In Egypt the River Nile flooded at this time of year and lions came from the desert to drink. Ever since that time, the lion's head has often been used on fountains, as you have probably seen in many parks.

The tail of *Leo* ends with a star called *Denebola*, but legend says that it once ended with the cluster of stars visible above *Denebola*. This cluster, which you can see higher in the sky, is called *Berenice's Hair*, after the Egyptian queen who sacrificed her hair to the gods in gratitude for her husband's safe return from war. The king was angry until a priest pointed out that the gods had placed it in the sky. Fortunately, perhaps, for the priest, this made the king happy.

Leo – the Lion and star plan.

DENEBOLA

REGULUS

The two Bears

The best known group of stars in the sky is probably the *Plough*. Another popular name for it is the *Dipper* because it looks like a soup ladle. An old English name for it is *Charles' Wain* (or wagon).

The seven stars of the *Plough* are only part of the constellation of *Ursa Major – the Great Bear*. This and its companion, *Ursa Minor – the Little Bear*, never set in the latitude of the British Isles, so here they can be seen on every clear night of the year. In the late April evenings you must look for them, especially the *Great Bear*, high in the northern sky. An old Greek legend tells of two bears being placed in the sky by the god Jupiter. The jealous goddess, Juno, went to Neptune, the god of the sea, and asked him to refuse them the right to bathe in the deep, green waters of his sea-kingdom. Since then, the two bears have always been kept away from the horizon and the sea.

The constellation of the *Little Bear* contains the *Pole Star*. All the other stars in the sky seem to move around the *Pole Star*, but this is really because our earth is rotating on its axis. Actually, the direction of the earth's axis is very slowly changing and, in centuries to come, our world will have other 'Pole Stars'.

The second star from the end of the *Dipper's* handle is called *Mizar*.

(above) The Little Bear (Ursa Minor), (below) The Great Bear (Ursa Major) which includes the Plough (shown in yellow). The dotted line points to the Pole Star (Polaris) which can always be lined up from the two end stars of the Plough.

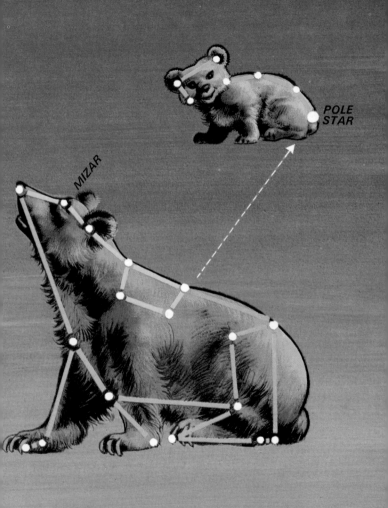

MIZAR

POLE STAR

May

The weather in May is frequently uncertain, but when the sky clears there are some interesting star-groups to be seen.

Virgo – the Virgin

At this time of year, the zodiac constellations are lower in the southern sky than in the winter, but you should have no problem in finding the stars of *Virgo*. Shown opposite you will see a picture of the young lady, though the arrangement of the stars also suggests a sailing ship; part of the constellation is, in fact, sometimes called '*Spica's Spanker*'. This is because the brightest star, *Spica* – and four others above it – form a shape like a spinnaker, a sail known to yachtsmen.

Virgo was said to represent the ancient corn-goddess, Persephone. In the old folklore of England she was also the 'kern-baby', a figure made from the last corn-stalks of the harvest field.

Earlier still, *Virgo* was said to be the goddess, Ishtar, who went down into the Underworld to find her husband, Tammuz, after he had been slain by winter in the shape of a wild boar. As she went, the whole earth fell under the spell of winter and nothing could grow. At last, the gods sent a messenger to the Underworld, pleading for Ishtar's return. She was set free. Her husband, Tammuz, came back with her, and slowly new life returned to the dark and frozen earth.

Virgo – the Virgin and star plan.

SPICA

Hercules

Although *Hercules* is not such a brilliant constellation as that other giant figure, *Orion – the Hunter*, he covers a very large part of the southern sky in the evenings of late spring and summer. Old star maps show him hanging head downwards, with one foot resting on the head of *Draco – the Dragon*, above. In this picture he is shown in a more comfortable, upright position and his brightest star, called *Ras Algethi*, an Arabic name, marks his left foot which is on our right as we face him.

Hercules is the subject of many old legends. One of them tells how he won his freedom from slavery by performing some very difficult and dangerous tasks, the twelve labours of Hercules. He had to face some terrifying adversaries, including a savage lion and a reptile with nine heads, the Hydra. Another of his tasks was to clean out the stables of King Augeas, where three thousand oxen lived and which had been neglected for many years.

The four stars shown at his head in the picture are sometimes called the *Keystone*, because they make a shape like the middle stone in the arch of a bridge. Near the upper left-hand star, at a point near the crown of his head, you may be able to see a faint, misty spot if the sky is very clear. This is a famous star-cluster in which the stars seem to be packed like a swarm of bees. But these thousands of sparkling suns are really far apart and they are so distant that their light takes more than thirty thousand years to reach us.

RAS
ALGETHI

June

Darkness comes late during June and the stars are not so brilliant as on winter evenings.

Libra – the Balance

To find the stars of *Libra – the Balance* (or the *Scales*), you must have a clear, unobstructed horizon for, like the other zodiac constellations of summer, this constellation stays low in the southern sky.

Libra is the only zodiac group which does not represent a living creature of some kind, human or animal. At one time it is believed to have formed a part of the next group, the *Scorpion*, but the Romans referred to this group as the *Scales* in memory of Julius Caesar, their Emperor, indicating his wisdom and justice.

An old Egyptian legend tells that the scales were those used by the god Osiris. Every man had his heart weighed against a feather when he died. Only if it proved lighter than the feather was he allowed into the land of the gods. This may suggest that feathers in those times must have been very heavy, or hearts very light, if any man was let in!

One of *Libra's* brighter stars, **Beta**, is unusual because of its pale green colour. This is not easy to see, for star colours are often very delicate.

Boötes – the Herdsman

The *Herdsman* is easily found, for this constellation rises high in the south and it has a shape rather like a great kite hanging in the sky. It also has a very brilliant, orange-coloured star, *Arcturus*, at the lower end.

(above) Libra – the Balance and star map,
(below) Boötes – the Herdsman.

BETA

ARCTURUS

Draco – the Dragon

If you have traced the two *Bears* in the northern sky, or the parts called the *Great Dipper* and the *Little Dipper*, you will find the winding stars of the *Dragon* curving their way between them.

In the Greek legend about Jason and the Golden Fleece, this was the dragon which kept guard over the golden apples in the garden of the Hesperides. In Egypt there were several temples built so that one of the *Dragon's* stars shone down upon the altar.

Corona Borealis – the Northern Crown

This little constellation really looks like its name. It may also be said to look much like a horseshoe. You will find it to the left of *Boötes* and its stars are quite bright. The Greeks used to call it the *Crown of Ariadne*, the princess from the island of Crete, for whom it was flung into the sky by the god Bacchus. Its brightest star is called *Alphecca – the Pearl of the Crown*, but is also known as Gemma.

Although the stars of the *Crown* form such a pleasing shape, they are not travelling together as some star-families do. In centuries to come, and as they move in different directions, the gems of Ariadne's crown will be scattered and star watchers will no longer recognise the constellation we now see.

(above) Draco – the Dragon and star map,
(below) – Corona Borealis – the Northern Crown
and star map.

ELTHANIN

THUBAN

GEMMA

July

For a few weeks in midsummer the night sky is not completely dark in the latitude of the British Isles. Twilight lasts all night. This may seem strange when one considers that, in early July, the earth is at its greatest distance from the sun, about three million miles more distant than it is in January. Here are some of the stars which you can see in the summer twilight.

Scorpio – the Scorpion

Like *Libra*, its neighbour in the zodiac, the *Scorpion* is very low in the southern sky and would be hard to find except for the brilliant, red star *Antares*. Its name means 'the rival of Mars', for the planet *Mars*, too, shines with a bright red light.

Antares is a star in the red giant class, but much cooler than the sun. *Antares* is so large that if it were in the same position as the sun, there would be no space for the earth or even some of the outer planets.

Perhaps it was because of the brilliant colour of *Antares*, like a red flame, that it was regarded as a sign of misfortune in some countries of the east, where it was called 'the Grave-digger of Caravans'.

The *Scorpion* was always supposed to be the enemy of *Orion – the Hunter*, and lies opposite to him in the sky.

The Milky Way runs down to the southern horizon through the *Scorpion*. There are many closely-packed star-clusters and the gas-clouds called nebulae in this part of the sky. Mostly, however, they are too near the horizon to be easily seen from Britain.

28   *Scorpio – the Scorpion and star map.*

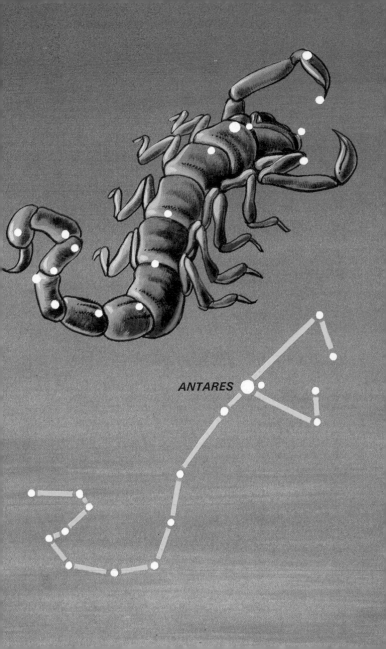

ANTARES

Ophiuchus and Serpens – the Serpent-holder and the Serpent

Above the *Scorpion* are two star-groups which, together, cover a very large part of the southern sky.

The picture of the Serpent-holder shows him as a man whose body is entwined by the coils of a huge snake. He is gripping the writhing creature in his hands.

Ophiuchus was said to have been a famous doctor named Aesculapius, who could restore even the dead to life. The god of the Underworld very much disliked his medical skill and persuaded Jupiter, father of the gods, to put him in the sky where he could be kept well away from his patients.

This is a vast and complicated group of stars, not easy to identify. It is difficult to see the form of a man, but the illustration opposite will help you to recognise the line of stars representing the Serpent. It will help if you have found the *Scorpion*, for the *Serpent-holder's* foot almost rests on the *Scorpion's* head, just above the bright red star, *Antares*.

The *Serpent-holder* and *Scorpion* are best seen in July though the *Scorpion* is always very low in the southern sky.

Ophiuchus – the Serpent-holder.

August

In August the nights are darker and it is easier to see the stars against a blacker sky.

Sagittarius – the Archer

The zodiac constellations are still low in the southern sky, so we need a clear horizon to find the stars of the *Archer*, who is one of the two Centaurs in the heavens. Centaurs were legendary creatures with a human head and torso and the body of a horse. Like its neighbour, the *Scorpion*, *Sagittarius* lies in the star-clouded stream of the Milky Way. One part of the constellation is the *Milk Dipper*, a group of stars shaped something like the *Plough*, or *Great Dipper*, in the northern sky.

Centaurs were common in old legends and the most famous of them was Chiron, who was supposed to have divided the stars into their constellation groups. The story says that he intended this one figure for his own likeness, especially to guide the Argonauts in their search for the Golden Fleece.

One day Chiron was accidentally wounded by an arrow from the bow of Hercules. The arrow had been dipped in the poison of the Hydra's blood. In his pain, Chiron cried out for Jupiter to let him die and Jupiter agreed to place him among the stars. But Chiron had divided out the sky so carefully in the north that there was now no room for him. He was sent to the far southern sky where he shines as the other Centaur, beyond our horizon.

Sagittarius – the Archer and star plan.

Aquila – the Eagle

High above the *Archer* flies *Aquila – the Eagle*, clearly marked by a short line of three bright stars with the brightest – *Altair* – in the middle.

One of the most delightful legends about *Aquila* includes the next constellation we shall look at, *Lyra – the Lyre*. The story tells of a cowherd and the spinning-maiden with whom he fell in love. The girl's father banished them to the sky, but they were allowed to meet once a year if they could cross the river of the Milky Way. Each year, on the seventh night of the seventh moon, they were able to do this, thanks to their friends, the magpies, who formed a feathered bridge for them to pass over. The next day the magpies returned to earth. You can see *Aquila*, representing the cowherd, and *Lyra*, marking the spinning-maiden, on either side of the pale band of the Milky Way.

Lyra – the Lyre

Immediately above *Aquila*, with its bright, middle star, *Altair*, is a very small constellation called *Sagitta – the Arrow*. Unlike many other groups it really looks like its name. Some distance above and to the right is the brilliant little form of the *Lyre*. In Britain it was sometimes called the *Harp of King Arthur*. In the Greek story it was the lyre of the god Orpheus, who so charmed the King of the Underworld that he agreed to restore to life, Eurydice, the lost bride of Orpheus. There was a condition that when Orpheus came for her, he should not look back, but, sadly he could not resist the temptation to take one brief glance behind him, only to see his fair Eurydice vanishing into the Underworld. The brilliant star in the *Lyre* is *Vega*.

(above) Aquila – the Eagle,
(below) Lyra – the Lyre and star plan.

ALTAIR

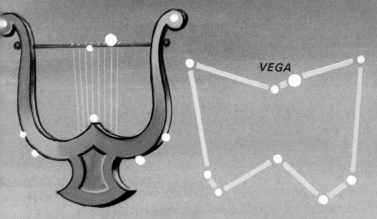

VEGA

September

September is the month of the harvest moon. This is also the month of the autumn equinox, meaning equal days and equal nights; daylight and darkness are both of twelve hours duration.

Capricornus – the Sea-goat

A large part of the southern sky which we see at this season was once thought of as a great sea. Several of the constellations we find there were said to represent a group of strange sea-creatures. The *Sea-goat* is one of them. It is rather low in the south, a straggling line of stars, beginning on the right with an interesting pair which are close together.

An old legend about the Sea-goat tells how the god Pan one day jumped into the River Nile. For the amusement of the onlookers he turned himself into a curious animal with the head of a goat and the tail of a fish. The illustration opposite shows you the stars of the *Sea-goat* and its shape.

The double star you can see at the western end is called *Gaedi*, an Arabic name meaning *the Kid*.

Delphinus – the Dolphin

The Dolphin is another of these strange sea-animals and you will see its sparkling, little diamond shape well above *Capricornus*, at the edge of the Milky Way. It is one of the most attractive small groups. The *Dolphin* comes into many old legends, but in Britain these stars were sometimes known as Job's Coffin.

(above) Delphinus – the Dolphin and star map, (below) Capricornus – the Sea-goat and star map.

GAEDI

Cygnus – the Swan

The stars of the *Swan* are also referred to as the *Northern Cross*. This is one of the most beautiful and well-marked star-groups in the sky. You will find it rising high overhead in the late September evening. It lies right in the track of the Milky Way and, if the night is very clear, you may notice that there is a division in the pale band of starlight. This is because some of the stars are hidden by dark clouds of dust and gas.

The shape of the *Cross* can be clearly seen. At the foot of the *Cross* (the beak of the Swan), is the star called *Albireo*. This name is said to mean the Chicken's Head and, in fact, the constellation was sometimes known as the *Hen*. If you have the opportunity to look at *Albireo* with a telescope you will find it divided into two separate stars. The larger one is a golden colour and the smaller one, close beside it, is blue. *Albireo* is often said to be one of the most attractive sights in the sky for the telescope user.

The brightest star in *Cygnus* is the one at the *Swan's* tail (the head of the *Cross*). Its name is *Deneb*, which is also given to some other stars belonging to animal constellations, and it means the tail.

A legend about *Cygnus* connects it with Phaethon, the son of Apollo who, for one day, drove the sun-chariot of his father. The daring act ended in disaster. Phaethon fell into a river. His devoted brother dived to recover his body and his graceful diving was rewarded when gods placed him in the sky in the form of the *Swan*.

Cygnus – the Swan and star plan.

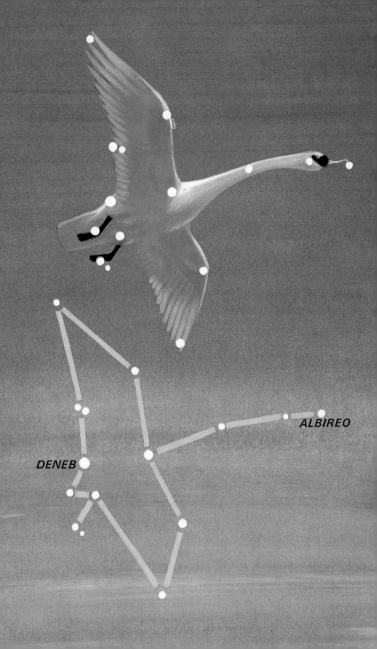

DENEB

ALBIREO

October

During this month there are sure to be some fine nights for looking at stars.

Aquarius – the Water-bearer

The illustration opposite shows the figure of *Aquarius* pouring out water from an urn into the mouth of a fish, far below him in the sky. This constellation lies next to the *Sea-goat*, but rises higher into the southern sky.

In Egypt, it was thought that the flooding of the River Nile was brought about by the *Water-bearer* dipping his urn as he filled it. Whether *Aquarius* was popular or unpopular seems to have depended very much upon where the ancient peoples lived. The *Water-bearer* was worshipped in dry lands where rain was rare and precious, but elsewhere, he was blamed for floods which sometimes ruined the crops.

One of the stars of this constellation has an Arabic name which means 'Luckiest of the Lucky', but is more usually named after the second letter of the Greek alphabet – *Beta*. It is a very large star, a supergiant like its neighbour, *Alpha* – named after the first letter of the Greek alphabet. Both are so far away that their light takes more than a thousand years to reach us.

The shape of *Aquarius* is not very clear, but you may easily find the stars of the urn. Very low, near the horizon, you may get a glimpse of the *Southern Fish* which catches the water. It is marked by a bright, lonely-looking star, *Fomalhaut*.

Aquarius – the Water-bearer and the Southern Fish.

ALPHA

BETA

FOMALHAUT

Pegasus – the Winged Horse

The part of this constellation which is easiest to find is the big square formed by four, bright stars, high in the southern sky.

Pegasus appears on old Greek coins which were in use about the year 500 BC. It was said that wherever the feet of Pegasus touched the ground, a spring of water poured from the footprint. One fountain, which legend says sprang from a high wall of rock when *Pegasus* touched it, can still be seen in Greece.

Henry Longfellow, an American poet, wrote a famous poem – Pegasus in Pound. He imagined Pegasus visiting a village in New England. The people flocked to see the strange animal with its wings and mane of gold. They put it in the village pound, the enclosure for stray animals, but the next day it had disappeared and, where it had been standing, they saw a spring of clear water gushing from the earth.

The star at the top of the Great Square of *Pegasus* is called *Alpheratz* and is shared by the neighbouring group of *Andromeda*. The one at the top right-hand corner is a vast, red giant star with a diameter over a hundred times greater than that of the sun.

Pegasus – the Winged Horse.

November

Astronomers often find that a little mist makes the air very steady and the stars do not twinkle so much.

Pisces – the Fishes

You will find the *Fishes* in the uneven line of stars which straggles beneath the Great Square of *Pegasus*, but they are less brilliant than the four which make up the Square.

The Greeks used to believe that the two fishes were Venus and Cupid, and that they were joined by a silver ribbon. They took on this disguise when, with other gods, they were threatened by the giant Typhon as they played beside the River Nile. Typhon was at last overcome by the father of the gods, Jupiter, who buried him beneath the rocks of Mount Etna on the island of Sicily.

Even then, says the legend, Typhon was liable to struggle for his freedom and his anger boiled over in the white-hot lava which sometimes flowed from the volcanic crater and down the mountain-side towards the villages below.

The stars of Pisces – the Fishes.

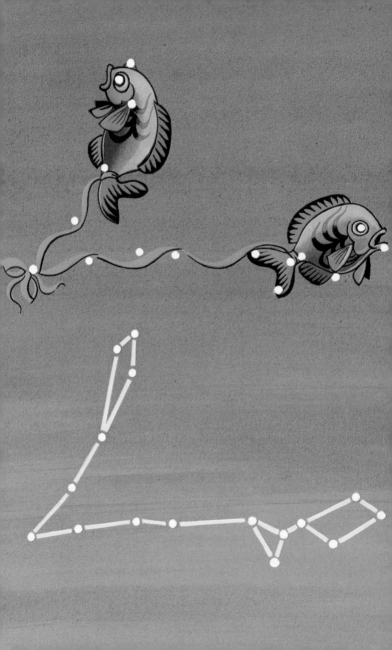

Andromeda and Perseus

The stars of *Andromeda* stretch eastwards in a line from the upper, left-hand corner of the Great Square of *Pegasus*. Where they curve into the Milky Way, you will find the stars of *Perseus*.

Andromeda was the daughter of King Cepheus and his queen, Cassiopeia, who are also in the sky not far away. Cassiopeia offended King Neptune by claiming that her daughter was more beautiful than any of Neptune's sea-nymphs. A monster, *Cetus*, whose stars are below those of the *Fishes*, was sent to avenge this insult. It was agreed, however, that the kingdom should be left unharmed if Andromeda herself were offered as a prey to the sea-monster.

Andromeda was chained to a rock, awaiting her fate, when the sound of a great wind reached her ears. Andromeda thought it must be the monster but it was the wings of the flying horse, Pegasus, with Perseus on his back. The sea-monster was quickly overcome. Perseus returned triumphant with his rescued princess and, years afterwards, Jupiter gave them all an honoured place among the stars.

The faint patch of light in *Andromeda*, where the *Great Andromeda Galaxy* lies, is a vast, spiral system of thousands of millions of stars. It is the only one of the far-off galaxies which can be seen with the unaided eye. A small telescope or a pair of binoculars will bring it into view quite clearly. To see it with the naked eye you must look for it on a very clear night. You may see it better if you turn your eye slightly to one side while keeping your attention on the right spot. Faint objects can often be seen by this trick.

The map will show you where the Galaxy can be found, a little way above the main stars of the *Chained Maiden*. Below this line, facing north, you will see the diamond form of *King Cepheus* and the *W*-shape of *Cassiopeia, the Lady in the Chair*.

ALGOL

GALAXY

December

The last month of the year brings the shortest day and long, dark evenings for looking at the stars. Much wondering and many calculations have failed to give us any satisfactory explanation about the Star of Bethlehem seen by the Wise Men. We still know no more about it than the Gospel of St. Matthew tells us. Here are some of the stars you can see this month. They were shining over Bethlehem too, at the time of the first Christmas.

Aries – the Ram

The Ram comes first in the following verse, written by the hymn-writer, Isaac Watts, which lists the twelve constellations of the zodiac:

> The Ram, the Bull, the Heavenly Twins,
> And next the Crab the Lion shines,
> The Virgin and the Scales;
> The Scorpion, Archer and Sea-goat,
> The Man who pours the water out
> And Fish with glittering tails.

Legend says that when the gods were driven from their home on Mount Olympus, in Greece, and took refuge in Egypt, the ram was the disguise chosen by Jupiter to escape from the giant Typhon. *Aries* was also identified as the ram whose golden fleece was sought by Jason and the Argonauts.

The stars of *Aries* are few and they lie on a short, curved line some distance below the constellation of *Andromeda*. Between the two is another little star-group called *Triangulum – the Triangle*, a shape you will easily discover although the stars are not very bright. The *Ram's* most prominent star is called *Hamal*, the Arabic word for a sheep.

Aries – the Ram and star plan.

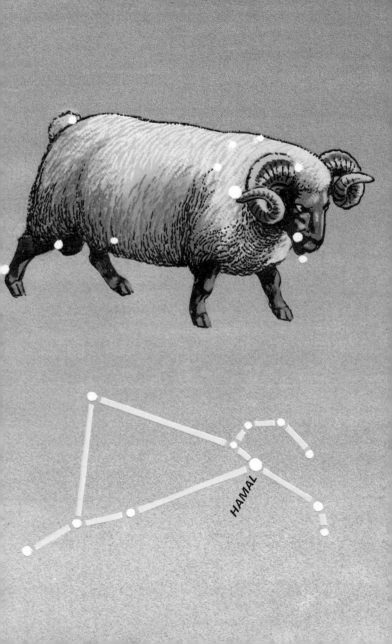

HAMAL

Cetus – the Whale

Like some of the constellations already described, *Cetus – the Whale* or the *Sea-monster*, belongs to the mythical sea-region of the heavens. You will probably look in vain for anything which really resembles a whale, and the zig-zag line of stars lies rather low in the southern sky this month, some distance below the *Fishes*.

This is the creature which legend says threatened to devour the *Chained Maiden*, *Andromeda*, but there are stories which suggest that *Cetus* was regarded as some kind of gigantic sea-animal even before the legend of Andromeda and Perseus was told.

The most interesting star in the *Whale* is one which is called *Mira*, a name meaning the wonderful star. It was given by an astronomer named Fabricius in the year 1596, when he discovered that the light of the star changes in a strange way. It stays at its brightest for about ten days and then begins to fade slowly. The fading light takes as long as seven months until it cannot be seen by the naked-eye. After a short time it begins to brighten over a period of three months. The entire change takes nearly a year and we cannot yet explain why it behaves in this unusual way. *Mira* remains a mystery star nearly four hundred years after the keen-eyed, David Fabricius first detected its slowly-winking light.

Cetus – the Whale and star plan.

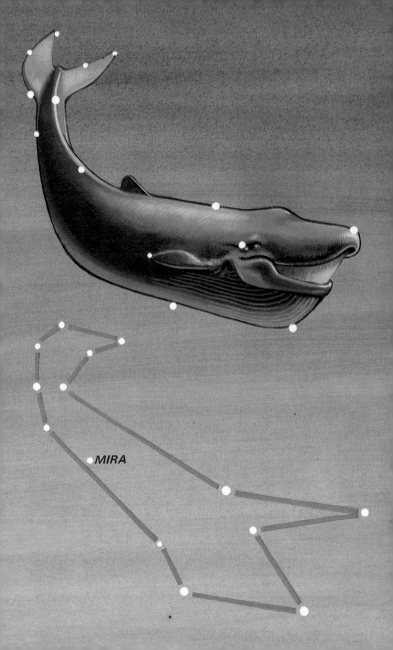

MIRA

THE STARS IN AUTUMN

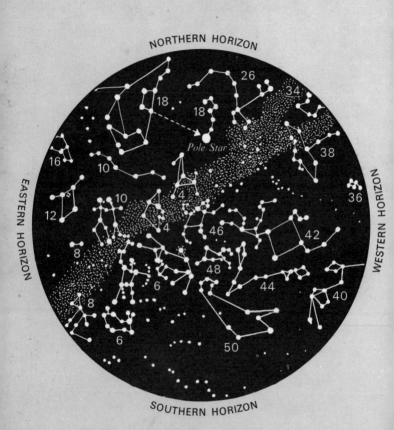

NORTHERN HORIZON

Pole Star

EASTERN HORIZON

WESTERN HORIZON

SOUTHERN HORIZON